The People's His

Around Meadow Well

by

Pat Hope

To Joyce
Best Wishes
Pat Hope.

A group of residents on a week's holiday at Iona, an island off the west coast of Scotland in 1997. Cedarwood Trust takes a group of people every year to Iona. Left to right: Jenny Lancaster, Robert Michael, Brian Abdullah, Dennis Marsh, Elaine Andrews, Annette Smith, Reverend David Peel and Joanne Belfon.

Previous page: George Bean and his mam Elizabeth, outside their home on Oakwood Avenue in 1955. George was on leave from the Regular Army. He joined the Army in 1954 and trained as a Artillery Gunner. In the early days of my youth I remember the mothers wearing aprons with bibs attached. They are rarely seen today.

Copyright © Pat Hope 2000

First published in 2000 by

The People's History Ltd
Suite 1
Byron House
Seaham Grange Business Park
Seaham
Co. Durham
SR7 0PY

ISBN 1 902527 72 0

Contents

The May Procession was held at St Joseph's RC Church on Wallsend Road in 1950. The Procession was held on May Day and had been a tradition for many years. In 1936, huge crowds of people gathered and lined the streets outside the church hours before the procession began. The church was decorated with bunting and the papal flag flew from the roof. Heading the long line of 400 children were the cross bearers and acolytes. The boys with white shirts and red sashes and the boys from the Parish in ordinary clothing. After them came the girls in white dresses and veils and the girls from the Parish. The banner of the Children of Mary was carried by the President. Miss Martin came next with the holy angels bedecked with white veils, gold braid ribbons and medals. Behind them, came the Aspirants wearing white veils, blue ribbons and medals, and a plaster statue of Our Blessed Lady adorned with flowers. The May Queen was dressed in white satin, with a white embroidered veil and a magnificent train, two and a half yards long, made in white chiffon velvet, lined with blue satin and trimmed with gold braid and ermine. The brides of honour were in dresses of white satin. They wore white veils.

Introduction

When I was asked to split the information I had gathered over the years, on the history of Chirton and Meadow Well, I was horrified. I must stress that this book is not the history of Meadow Well, it is an account in photographs of true community spirit.

My search of the Meadow Well began with an initial letter to North Tyneside Library Local Studies for information in May 1994. Then in the first year of the Millennium I was asked to collect photographs of people. I found a number of people who were all too happy to lend me them. My family, who grew up here in the 1930s and '50s, were also helpful.

Our families, neighbours and friends are unique. They are fighters for the truth and their beliefs. For some people, neighbours take the place of family. We take care of one another and are a close-knit community.

Besides the hardship of war and the decline of work, Meadow Well's past has had many happy memories and the people never gave up hope. I myself have lived, with my family, on the estate for twenty years and I have found a wealth of sociability. I have found that the people of Meadow Well are welcoming and friendly to one another.

There are four men I am grateful to, besides my husband; without them, this book would not exist. Alan Hildrew, from North Tyneside Library Local Studies, has been a good friend to have. The phone calls and letters Alan received, where he's researched the information I've needed, are too numerous to count. Steve Conlan, from Waterville Detached Project, has helped me to scan the photographs on computers. His love for photography can been seen in much of his work. He has been a major part in the project since 1994. David Peel, our pastoral priest, who has dedicated his life in helping the people of Meadow Well. He has supported the project financially and with interest. Last but not least, Andrew Clark, who has worked hard to finalise this book for it to become a rewarding and picturesque publication.

The information in this book was given to me in good faith but there is no guarantee of absolute accuracy. I hope, you the reader, has as much pleasure looking over the photographs in this book as I have had in both collecting and selecting them. Finally, the friends who are no longer with us, I dedicate this book.

Pat Hope

A Brief History

In the sixty years plus of the Meadow Well Estate, formerly the Ridges, there have been four generations, the fifth is now being born. The estate today has altered immensely since it originated.

In 1934 families, with their belongings, were relocated to the estate from the Fish Quay slums. In the 1930s and '40s, standards of life were simple and primitive. The lack of resources kept the folk in hardship. Their main meal of the day was a varied diet of vegetable stew, leek pudding, potatoes and suet dumplings – economic and easy to come by, yet high in carbohydrate. Meat was a luxury item and rarely affordable. During the war, meat was difficult to buy except through rationing. Breakfast and supper consisted of bread and dripping or bread and condensed milk.

Clothing for the children was mostly hand-me-downs, from the oldest to the youngest or received from friends and neighbours. Knitting was a pastime, making cardigans, jumpers and socks. Another pastime was when the families made clippy mats. They used strips of material and sewed them together. Many homes had linoleum on the floor and the mats were made to decorate the home.

Household cleaning was done with a galvanised bucket and carbolic soap. Washing for a large family was with tablets of green soap with poss-tubs and sticks, washboard and a rubber roller table mangle. The mothers always had time to wash their front door steps, using a yellow rubbing stone or pumice stone. Families with red steps were classed as better-off.

The homes that were flats, had back to back fire and oven. The fire was in the front room and oven in the scullery. They cooked, boiled kettles and heated irons on the top part of the oven.

War began in September 1939 and the Council built temporary air-raid shelters, built with bricks and corrugated iron sheets. Public shelters were on Front Street, Silkey's Lane, Howdon Road and Waterville Road for those who were caught short from home. Fathers and brothers were called up and mothers and sisters of working age helped keep the country intact. Identification cards were issued for every member of the community. Ration books were also used for food in short supply.

The estate had a fair share of bombs, hitting Smith's Park, Silkey's Lane, Collingwood Field, the corner of West Percy Road, the middle of Maple Crescent, Waterville Road and the Ridges Council School. The homes seriously damaged by enemy action were demolished and rebuilt, the families were rehoused.

Open-air dancing was held in Smith's Park in June and July 1943; from Thursday to Friday, from 7.30 pm to 10 pm for four weeks. First class concerts were held on the Thursday evenings, with N. Moutrey and his Hawaiian Swingtet as well as the Hotspurs and the King Jesters. Families from all around the area came to see them. On the 18th June to the 3rd July 1943, 'Holidays at Home', came to the estate and the Grand Amusement Fair on Collingwood Field was held. From the 5th to the 10th July 1943, the Reco Brothers Empire Circus was held on the field.

In the early hours of 7th May 1945, the Germans signed an unconditional surrender. It took almost half a day before the news was announced over Britain. Glad tidings spread across the estate like an infectious disease. It was a day all Britain had hoped for, but feared might never come. They cried with joy and the church bells rang. Everyone got together and prepared for a Victory Tea Party. They were held in Briarwood Avenue, West Percy Road, Peartree

Crescent, Waterville Road, Linden Road, Limewood Road, Hazelwood Avenue, Rowan Avenue, Cedarwood Avenue, Bridge Road, Appletree Gardens, Dahlia Gardens and Woodlea Crescent, from the Sunday 13th May to the Saturday 19th May 1945. A wind-up gramophone was brought out and games were organised for the children when the tea was cleared away. A knees-up was followed for the adults. The street lights were turned on for the first time since 1939.

Clothes rationing continued until 1949. Women walked around stockingless, a pair took up a valuable coupon. Many drew fake stocking seams up their legs with liquid leg make-up. Food rationing ended in 1953.

Many families suspended their door key with string at the back of the front door. Everyone helped and trusted each other. Break-ins were unheard of. In general, the estate had modern day facilities and spacious gardens. The streets were named after trees.

In 1969 a ten-point plan was devised by Councillor Charles Carter to clean up the estate. The Council moved the residents out, street by street and stripped the houses bare. The official name of the estate changed to Meadow Well, then in 1972 many of the street names changed.

In 1991 there was much unrest on the estate. Two years later, partly as a result of the City Challenge and the Royal Quays Development, more changes were underway, to add another chapter to the short but eventful life of this estate.

The Celtic Knott on Waterville Road is the centre point of the estate. It was completed in 1998. The Architect involved won a British award for the best design.

Acknowledgements

I would like to thank the following people for their kind permission and co-operation. Without them, this book would not exist.

Peter Hope
Joseph Rippeth
Grace Nathan
Linda Nathan
Jean Bean
Dave Henderson
Linda Graham
William Bridges
Michael Hope
Margaret Nolan
Michael Marsh
Ethel Walker

Ellen Heads
Patricia Appleton
Irene Verte
Mick Tait
John Crow
Elizabeth Bean
Ruth Burgess
Theresa Maholme
Helen Ball
Maxenne Ball
Paul Charters
Karen Hackworth

Annette Wind
Mick Thompson
Maria Marsh
Marianne Pentz
Diane Michael
Margaret (Peggy) Morgan
Maureen Williamson
Derrick Cowley (Decka)
Amanda Nathan
Steve Elliot

Alan Hildrew, Local Studies, North Tyneside Library.
Eric Hollerton, Local Studies, North Tyneside Library.

Steve Conlan, Photographer, Waterville Detached Project.

Reverend David Peel, Cedarwood Trust.
Reverend Shiela Auld, Cedarwood Trust.
Reverend Charles Hope, Minister for Percy Main.
Canon Alec Barrass, Minister for St Joseph's Church.
Sister Michael, Headmistress for St Joseph's School.
Tony Patterson, Photographer, North Shields People's Centre.
Edward Graveling, The Square Building Trust.
Richard Potts, Tyne and Wear Archives.
Elizabeth Rees, Tyne and Wear Archives.
Mrs Duncan, Headmistress, Waterville Primary School.
Sharon Barker, Housing Manager N.T.C.
Dave Garnish, Education Department (North Tyneside).
Carol Wark, The Meadows Children's Project.

I would also like to thank the shop owners and workers who posed for the camera.

Published in association with North Tyneside Libraries.

STREETS AND BUILDINGS

An aerial view of the Ridges Estate, during 1938-1939. Several homes were not yet built at this time, the last phase of building was completed in 1939. The Ridges public house was completed in 1940. The Ridges Reservoirs were in use at the time, until the latter part of the 1950s.

Meadow Well Farm in the 1890s. The farm was sold through auction in 1869 to the Duke of Northumberland. It contained three cottages with outbuildings and an excellent 'Well' of water. Compulsory Purchase Order was served in October 1932, by Tynemouth Borough Council, to make way for the erection of the new Ridges Estate.

The first record of the Vicarage on Wallsend Road and Waterville Road was 1865, held by the Reverend Arthur Tomline Coates. The Vicarage had a yearly value of £300 in the gift of the Duke of Northumberland. Reverend Coates was vicar for 32 years, until he died in 1897. In December 1956 it was sold to the brewery and converted into a public bar and lounge, named The Redburn.

Tynemouth Borough Council Committee Inspection in 1933. They are standing on the first phase of building on the Ridges Estate. This area of building was completed in November 1933.

The interior of 11 Magnesia Bank, on the Bankside in 1933. These were the conditions many residents endured before they moved on to the estate. The Medical Officer at that time reported upon the unhealthy, insanitary and dilapidated state of the buildings. They washed, ate and slept in the same room. Before they moved on the estate residents were taken to Moorside Hospital and were bathed and deloused. Their belongings, including furniture, were passed through a fumigation chamber.

Mr & Mrs Robert W. Brown and their family, inside their home on Laburnum Avenue in the 1950s. Jean, sitting first on left, had just finished work at Tyne Brand on the Fish Quay. Sitting round the table in the front room for their meals was traditional on the estate. It was the warmest room in the flat.

Left: Sitting in the front garden on deck chairs on West Percy Road in 1955: Mrs Bell, Karen Rippeth and her grandmother, Grace Rippeth. All homes on the estate were flats and had metal-framed windows.

An Easter gathering of grandchildren on West Percy Road in 1960. Grandfather, Joseph Rippeth is with Lesley Ann Wallis (baby in the pram), Ann Sprouston (left) and Karen Rippeth (right). The gardens were quite small to accommodate the blocks of flats. Each street on the estate has a line of trees at the side of the road.

Marina Avenue in the early 1960s. This was the centre point of the estate, to hear any gossip and, of course, buy their daily provisions. N. & F.M. Gibson sold wool and haberdashery. John Day was the fruit and vegetable shop. There was also a Children's Library and Thompson's Red Stamp Store. The space between the buildings was built into a shop and flat, owned by Hoult's pork shop.

Steven Bean posed for the camera outside his grandparents home on Laburnum Avenue in 1971. Behind him, the shops on Marina Avenue. From 1969 to 1971, the estate was revitalised, and the official name was changed to 'Meadow Well'. Following this up in 1972 with many of the street names being changed.

A couple of friends meeting each other at the bottom of Oakwood Avenue in 1959. Take a look at the bicycles? Many gardens were not used at this time, only the faithful ones kept their garden tidy. The boys found it hard to find employment, yet the girls worked as shop assistants or in factories. The leaving school age at this time was fifteen.

George Bean standing on the corner house on Laburnum Avenue in 1957.
Across the right side are Marina Avenue and West Percy Road. Many families
were coming to grips with the end of rationing from war-time and the new
craze of teddy boys and bopping.

Around 1950 on the corner of Waterville Road and Dahlia Gardens, a group of
children posed for the camera. Back: Annette Wind and Irene Nicholson.
Front: Patrick Wind, Valerie Nicholson and George Johnson. Behind them
stands the Ridges Inn. It was the first licensed premises on the estate and
opened its doors for business on 16th April 1940, owned by William McEwan
and Company Limited, a Scottish brewer.

The Grotto in the grounds of St Joseph's School and Church around the 1950s. I have been told the Madonna is still on display but the rail etc has been removed from this spot. Many residents had spiritual guidance and a place of worship when times were hard.

St Joseph's Catholic Church and Parish Hall in the 1950s. The Parish Hall was actually a temporary church, opened in May 1935. The new Parish Hall was built and blessed in December 1936.

The Barn in 1991. The children from Collingwood Youth Club used the building for playing activities. It was once the home for the keeper at the Ridges Reservoirs. The Census Returns of 1861 states Mr & Mrs James Hall were residing at the Ridges Cottage. It was demolished after extensive damage during the 1991 riots.

Collingwood Youth Club in 1991. The foundations were laid for the club in 1966 and the building was completed in July 1967. It was built on stilts as they were afraid it might subside into the reservoir. The leaders in the beginning were George Ryan and George Williamson. Play leader was Dave Hood. Downstairs was built around 1981. During the riots of 1991 the youth club burned down and had to be demolished.

A queue stretched out from Cedarwood Avenue to Bridge Road South. From pensioners to young families with children, they were all waiting for their share of free butter. At the time there was huge butter mountains. (Courtesy: Steve Conlan, from *The Independent Magazine*, 5th January 1991.)

Good Friday in 1962, Patricia (8) and sister Linda Nathan (7) posing for the camera with their new Easter clothes. The trees lining West Percy Road were a familiar picture on the estate. At the top of the road was the playing fields and grounds of Ralph Gardner School. Later that year their granda died and the girls no longer visited his home on West Percy Road.

Smith's Dock War Memorial, dated 25th July 1922. It was built in memory of the men who worked for Smith's Docks and died, fighting for King and Country, during the First World War. Smith's Park, where the memorial stands, was flattened in 1995 to make way for the new sports centre and grounds. Chirton Dene Park was developed between the grounds. Bridge Road South and Howdon Road border the grounds.

Apartments in Murray Close on the westside of the estate in 1995. The flats today have been refurbished and sold to private owners. This area was once a riverbed for the Red Burn. It flowed from Murton Row to the River Tyne, passing through a quiet retreat named Coble Dene. The Red Burn carried a fine red percipitate.

In 1994, a derelict building of a burnt out shell from the riots of 1991. It was originally the Marina fish shop. The shop and flat in Avon Avenue was owned by Ashfaq Ahmed who jumped for his life from an upstairs window when a mob petrol-bombed the premises.

Cedarwood Avenue Centre. The glass Mosaics were put together by the local residents on the estate in the 1990s. The centre was situated at 23 Cedarwood Avenue on the South Meadow Well. It began in September 1980, with two workers, a social worker and a nurse.

St Joseph's Roman Catholic Church. The photograph was taken in 1995. St Joseph's Church on Wallsend Road was consecrated in August 1955, by His Lordship the Right Reverend Joseph McCormack, Lord Bishop of Hexham and Newcastle. The architect was Mr Burke. The church is a modern expression of the traditional Gothic style, in brick of Autumn gold and artificial stone. The church is a 110 feet long and 43 feet wide. The height in the nave is 33 feet.

St John's Church of England in Percy Main. The photograph was taken in 1997. St John's Church was consecrated in September 1864, by the Lord Bishop of Durham. The church was built of stone in the early English style. The first incumbent was the Reverend Arthur Tomline Coates BA, who lived at the Vicarage on Wallsend Road.

The Meadow Well Clinic on Waterville Road in 1994. The clinic was built on the old reservoir site. The official opening was on 29th October 1982 by Mrs Sylvia M. Murray CBE, Chairman of North Tyneside Health Authority. Part of the original reservoir wall still exists today. It is the only bit of history remaining on the estate.

The Meadows Community Centre on Waterville Road in March 1995. The centre was built by the Meadowell Construction Company on the old reservoir site and was officially opened on 1st October 1994. In 1996 an extension was built. It includes: Hunter's Cafe (named after Norman Hunter) run by voluntary trainees for staff and the public alike; offices and I.T. room; crafts room; crèche and a hall. The centre has now introduced courses for the residents – from education to 'Into Work' opportunities.

The Meadow Well Neighbourhood and Childcare Centre on Avon Avenue in 1994. The centre was officially opened in July 1993 by John Foster, Executive Director for North Tyneside Council. The workers have their own selected teams: Customer Services, Housing, Into Work. There is also a crèche, for the youngsters up to 3 years. The centre is for paying Rents and Council Tax, and they deal with any queries, complaints and repairs. They are a service to the community.

The Meadow Well Metro Station on Bridge Road in February 1995. The station was officially opened on 7th November 1994 by Councillor Roy Burgess BEM, Chairman of the Tyne and Wear Passenger Transport Authority. The original name was Smith's Park Station. It has quite a pleasant appearance – bright in the cold winter months and on a dark rainy day.

Renovations on Ripley Avenue in January 1995. The renovations for the whole estate began in 1993, starting at Bridge Road South, partly as a result of the City Challenge and the Royal Quays Development. The year 2000 has seen the completion, with more changes underway to add yet another chapter to the short but eventful life on this estate.

The construction in 1996, of the new sports centre, On the official opening the centre was named – The Parks. Minton Lane faces the rear of the building. Soon after, the houses on Minton Lane were renovated, to blend in with the new Childcare Centre and sports centre, bowling greens, tennis courts, football courts and Chirton Dene Park nearby.

Celtic Knott in 1998. The architect involved won an award for the design. May of that year was a hectic month for the nearby families. The men worked seven days a week with the noise from the drills and saws, and dust flying. The work disrupted pedestrians leaving the metro station and the traffic on Waterville Road. It was not long after that the nearby families enjoyed their weekends in peace.

Waterville Road in 1995. A young boy was riding his bicycle along this road, when he was hit by a car and died. There were demonstrations along the road for measures to calm the traffic to be brought in. This wish was granted.

A young girl called Laurie Joyce sitting with her panda and dog on a warm summer's day on Malton Crescent. On the estate, this was a view many families had to endure; boarded up houses. Yet, as families moved out, the Council had to board them up for any vandalism. Quite a few have been demolished.

An aerial view of Chirton Dene Water Park, in the first stages in November 1992. Chirton Dene has ran continually along the same route for centuries to the River Tyne. Before the Albert Edward Dock came into existence in 1884, it was a quiet retreat for town dwellers. Both the Red Burn and Chirton Dene met at Coble Dene, a wooded ravine, teeming with buttercups and sea daisies, and a shallow bed of rounded pebbles close to the River Tyne. It's said, the speckled trout once slumbered beneath the stones of the Dene. Yet, it was fouled with pit pumps continually pouring out its dirt, after 1811, when the pits were opened. Today, the park, starts at Minton Lane, under the bridge on Howdon Road, to the Royal Quays Marina.

WORK AND ARMED FORCES

The start of work on the Tonbridge Playsite in 1986, formerly the Council Yard on Ash Road. The northside of the estate was crying out for a park or playing area for the children.

Isabella Rippeth, conductress and her co-driver for the Northern General Bus Company. She worked from 1954 to the beginning of the 1960s. There were two bus services from the depot on Norham Road – Tynemouth Bus Company and the Wakefield Bus Company. Her number was AA2496 while she was employed there. The depot still runs, under the name of Go Coastline, Go-Ahead Northern.

Isabella Reid Rippeth standing outside the Puroh Bakery on Waterville Road in 1953. Isabel worked at the bakery for four years, preparing pastry, cakes and bread.

The workforce standing outside the Puroh Bakery. The bakery closed down around 1965.

A Council employee for North Tyneside Council and People and Places standing on Hunter's Close, around 1994-1995. People and Places was an organisation run by Mrs Carol Bell on Avon Avenue. At the time The Green Machine shared the same building. The Green Machine was a business hiring garden equipment and selling plants. It was run by Dennis Marsh. Both Carol and Dennis have lived on the estate for most of their lives.

Charles Clay's workforce outside the factory on Norham Road in July 1956. West Chirton Trading Estate began from 1938, building factories along one side of Norham Road. The first recorded entry in the area was 1825, when Michael Robson Esquire resided in West Chirton Hall and 111 acres of land. A plantation surrounded the Hall. The Hall was a plain building built with brick. The Borough Council came into possession of the estate in August 1938, and 6-8 acres of land was reserved for educational purposes.

Charles Clay clothing factory on Norham Road in 1972. Two of their employees from Meadow Well are Ellen Heads and Sandra Rutter. At this time many school leaving age girls trained as machinists at Clay's factory. A number of married women of all ages brought a second wage into the family unit. They found the work was straight forward and friendly with the clothing in their price range, which all women are attracted to.

Below: Charles Clay clothing factory on Norham Road in 1958 had their work's dance at the Bath Assembly Rooms in Tynemouth. The Bath was a frequent place for all work occasions and weekly evening dances. Only a few full names are known: Ellen Heads, Mary Bell and Ossie Armin. The other names are known only by their first names: Mary, Margaret, Brenda and another Mary.

The Information Shop on the corner of Avon Avenue in 1989. The Information Shop was a boost to the estate. Many families were helped with DHSS forms, claims and also to what they were entitled to. Help with the household bills and any other information they required was provided. Denise Riach (standing), Dennis Marsh (sitting) and Amanda (with a pile of work on her lap), are inside the Information Shop in 1989.

The opening of the Credit Union at 79 Ripley Avenue in 1987. From left: Colin Whinny, Nancy Escritt, Nancy Peters and Ann Devine. Nancy Peters is a well-respected and active person on the estate. She has fought tooth and nail to get the estate back on its feet. Her ambition is to have a strong and healthy estate.

Horsham Grove Community Centre on the corner of Horsham Grove and Barmouth Way in 1992. Martin Craig is standing on the right. The occasion was a get-together for local residents, organisations and police to give their suggestions or ideas to help the nearby streets with their problems.

A number of children enjoying their work in the front garden at the Meadows Community Centre on Waterville Road in 1996-98. The children are: Samatha Richardson, Natalie Smith, Amy McVie and her twin sister Katie, Michael Grant, Mikey Pederson and Samantha Graham.

The Meadow Well Construction Company in 1994. They constructed the Community Centre (The Meadows) on Waterville Road. Their construction team continued to build. Their own building was next to the centre on Meadow Way. From right to left, front row sitting: Lee Morris, Micky Lowdon and Alan Welsh. Back row: Jimmy Brunton, Jason McNulty, Tony Brown and John Smith.

The Meadowell Construction Company preparing the foundations for the new Community Centre in 1993. The area was the old reservoir site on Waterville Road and next to the Meadow Well Clinic.

A group of workers outside Hoult's Pork Shop on Avon Avenue, July 2000.
From right: Sandra Fulton, Mrs Emily Hoult MBE, Christine Graham and Joan
Main. Emily Hoult came on to the estate in the 1950s with her husband and
opened the butcher's shop. The Pork Shop that stands behind the workers was
built and opened to the public in the early 1960s.

A group of workers outside Reilly's shop on Bridge Road South, July 2000.
Front, from right: Helen Reilly, Anna Marie Roadment and Sharon Denley.
Back: Jordan Reilly and Darren Porter.

In 1999 a local business, Tarmac, renovated the old children's library on Avon Avenue into the new drop-in centre. It is now the Cedarwood Trust.

Ayesha and Shakir Mahmood on Avon Avenue in September 2000. Shakir's shop opened in 1992 and was the first self-service shop after the riots in 1991. He sells everything you could name and opens early in the morning and closes at 9-30 pm in the winter, 10-00 pm in summer. He is open everyday of the week including the Christmas and Easter holidays.

Above: Rose Cottage on Waterville Road was built when the area was nothing but farms. Mr Kumar and his family became owners of Rose Cottage in 1983. The shop supplies groceries, household products, a newsagent, tobacconist and wine and spirits. A typical corner shop with a friendly service. *Below*: Back row: Deepika, Sunita her mother and father Kuldip Sharma Kumar. Front: Adi and Isha.

The owners of Purvis Superstore on Bridge Road South, July 2000. Ian Purvis, his mother-in-law Dorothy Dixon and his wife, Dorothy Purvis. The family has been through turmoil, from aggravated burglary to physical assault on all of them. Yet, they carried on, holding their business and their livelihood together; keeping their prices low and running a Christmas Club for those who have a low budget. They love the area and the people of Meadow Well.

Maxenne Ball outside her business, the fruit and vegetable shop on Avon Avenue in June 2000. Linda Graham, a resident, peeps through the shop window. Maxenne helps and caters for the residents needs. She sells not just fruit and vegetables, but also sweets; a small number of groceries and pop; and a good variety of healthy plants.

Artillery Gunners in Colchester in 1957. Front row, on left, is George Bean. His home address was Laburnum Avenue. George joined the Army in 1954 and trained as an artillery gunner. Their base was at Colchester in Essex and he served for 2 years and 11 months, travelling abroad in this time.

Joseph Rippeth in his regimental gear, serving in the Black Watch in 1950. Joseph trained in the Argyle and Sutherland Highlanders in Inverness for about 6 months and then in the Black Watch. Joseph's home address was West Percy Road, Ridges Estate.

Seamen on the ship *British Adventure* in the late 1950s. Thomas Wright from Cedarwood Avenue is kneeling behind the lifebuoy while another local boy, Jimmy Myers, is kneeling on the right.

In 1945 Thomas Bean sent his thanks for his birthday on the back of this photography. Tommy was a local lad and joined the Merchant Navy, working on passenger liners at Southampton from 1953-1960.

The men who served on the HMS *Raleigh* in 1979. Philip Dunning, 4th from the left, top row, is a local lad. HMS *Raleigh* is a training establishment, situated in Torpoint in Cornwall. The crew usually train for about six weeks, before choosing their selected occupation and going on to more training in a different ship of their category. The names of every man are signed on the back of this photograph.

Mario Chapman, on leave from the Regular Army in the 1962. The streets behind him are Oakwood Gardens and Laburnum Avenue. A small portion of the lands were used for greenery, to spruce up the estate, like the one behind him. He was a sergeant in the Territorial Army, based at the Tynemouth Drill Hall.

The Royal Engineers in 1949. The soldiers were doing their National Service for the two year period. They stayed in Egypt for most of their service. Third row from back, 3rd from right is Thomas (Harry) Nathan. His home address was Silkey's Lane, Ridges Estate.

Outside The Meadows Community Centre on the 2nd September 2000, the cadets of Monkseaton Detachment Northumbria Army Cadet Force displaying equipment they use for training. The Army Cadet Force is one of the oldest uniformed youth organisations in the world. Both boys and girls may join from ages 13 years to 18 years 9 months. They are taught military skills, map reading, expedition skills and community work. Many take part in the Duke of Edinburgh's Award Scheme. Back row: Colour Sergeant Stu Lee, Cadet N. Brown, Cadet H. Carmichael, Lieutenant Ian Smith and Cadet Paul Silvester. (Ian and Paul live on the estate.) Front row: Cadet S. Ritchie, Cadet S. Harvey and Cadet R. Wall.

SPORTS AND PASTIMES

Western Primary School football team in June 1988. The following boys made up the football team. Back row, left to right: Christopher Wood, Mark Humes, Daniel Heslop, Games teacher, Mr Thornton, Brendon Teague, Paul ?, Lee Blythe and Gary Lemon. Front row: Joseph Elliot, Paul Fierney, Robert Gales, Steven Walker, Kevin Farelamb and Mark Walker. Western School has a long history. The school was once situated on Burdon Main Row and opened to the children (boys and girls were in separate schools) in 1972. The school at that time was called Western Board. They transferred to a new school on Waterville Road in September 1976. Western Primary was officially named in September 1981. In the same year, Infants and Juniors merged.

Western Primary School netball team in June 1988. Back row: Kerry Bishop; Denise Sunderland, Miss Ellenor (Games teacher), Jamie McDonald and Kelly Thompson. Front row: Sharon Wallis, Linda Dawson, Julie Slessor and Kerry Foster.

Meadow Well Primary School netball team in 1979. Back row: Jan ? , Tracy Dunning, Debbie Barbrooch, Kim Macauley and Mrs Rhena the games teacher. Front row: Susan Jackson, Mary Barber, Joanne Richardson, Helen Ball and Donna Linzy. Meadow Well School was once named the Ridges Day School. It was brought about by the development of the estate and the transference of families from the other parts of the town following on the slum clearance operations. The Education Committee decided to erect an infant school on

the estate. The Ridges Council School was officially opened on 20th October 1937, by the Mayor and Mayoress Councillor and Mrs A. Norman Park. One of their guests was Reverend John Clucas.

Waterville Primary School football team in 1980, with special guest, Sir John Hall at the back. Back row: Craig Hunn, Scott Walker, Mark Hunn, unknown, Carl Eden, Shaun Collins and Sean Thompson. Front row: Dean Walker, Jaye Pattern, ? Bowman, Martin Blythe, Aaron Carlson and Barry Aplynne. The headmaster was Tim Nicholson, who retired after 37 years in the educational service in 1981.

A netball event for two local schools in 1988. Western Primary School, from left, top row: Linda Dawson, Kelly Foster, Sharon Wallis, Kerry Bishop, Julie Slessor, Denise Sunderland and Kelly Thompson. Meadow Well Primary, from left, front row: 5th is Nichola Heron, 6th is Lisa Robinson. Both schools won a shield and certificates in the competition for teams in the area.

North Shields Boys' Club swimming group in the 1970s who were winners of
the County Swimming Championship. Front row: G. Horsborough, S. Williams,
D. Jamieson, David Heads and Keith Heads. Back row: K. Armstrong,
J. Broughton, A. Richardson and S. Sinclair.

A football team from Clelland's Shipyard in Willington Quay in the early
1980s. David Heads who lived on the estate with his parents, is 3rd left, in
back row. There are a number of boys who live on the estate all with a long-
lasting dream – to be a professional footballer for Newcastle United.

Mr Arthur Henry Marsh and his wife, Maria began learning Judo at the Trinity
Church Hall in Trinity Street in 1958. Their Judo career lasted two years, with
Arthur receiving his blue belt at
the age of 34. Maria receiving her
yellow belt at the age of 32. The
couple have lived on the estate all
their lives and have brought up a
large family.

Arthur Henry Marsh in the
Regular Army at Brancoath in
1948, at the age of 22 years. He
joined the Army in 1943 when he
was 17 years and left in 1950.

Collingwood Youth Club on
Waterville Road, around 1975-76.
Included are: Alan Balwin, Les
Cornforth, Paul Toby, ? Duffield,
William Glass, Christopher Badou,
Kevin Denley, Malcolm Lothian, Alan
Lockie, Paul Smith (Smidger), Trevor
Cook, Paul Bine (Basher), Paul Smith,
Norman Walker, Graham Denley,
James Toby and Thomas Culyer.

Right: Paul Charters, a local lad,
began his boxing career at the
Benfield Boys' Club in Walker in
1982. He had 75 fights, amateur and
professional. He won two Northern
Area Lightweight Championships,
fought in a British Illiminator and
competed for the European
Championship in Sicily. He is now a
trainer and provides his expertise to
professional boxers.

On West Percy Road in 1981, a game of football was played on a summer's day. All backs turned. From left: Michael Hope and his younger brother David in front of him. The boy in the middle is Graham Farnham and the man with long hair is Peter Hope.

Michael Marsh began his kick boxing career at Whitley Bay Boys' Club in 1993. His first amateur fight was against the British Champion after nine months of training. He received his black belt in 1998-1999. He won his British Champion Super Cruiserweight in 1997. In 2000, he is an assistant trainer to Steve Jessop at The Parks. His future ambition is to become a trainer for ages eight and over.

The Meadows Community Centre on Waterville Road had their Fun Day in 1999. The teams were formed by the centres and groups around the estate. Here we see the Council versus The Meadows in the Meadow Well Cup. The day brought many local people and children to The Meadows. They enjoyed the other activities that were on offer.

North Tyneside Council Housing selected a group of volunteers for their football team in 1999. They received a cup for playing at The Meadows, Meadow Well Cup Day. Back row: Lisa Barren (Housing Assistant Allocations), Marie Turner (Housing Officer Allocations) and Malcolm Young (Howdon Lettings). Front row: Neil Pool, Sharon Barker (Housing Manager) and Ian Wilkinson (Senior Housing Officer).

The Tonbridge
United football
team for the
under 12s and
under 13s in
1998. Mick
Thompson, a
local resident,
began his search
in 1998 for boys
who were
dedicated to
playing football.
Mick and the
teams since then
have gone from
strength to
strength, playing
teams in the
North Tyneside
area. Recently,
they played with
a group of boys
from Iona, while
staying there for
a week.

Tonbridge Play area in 1986. It was the former Council yard on Ash Road. The
estate's children enjoying their first experience on the slide. All too eager to try
it out from the look on their faces. The park had a variety of equipment but the
slide was the most popular.

RAF Crosby and Eden football team in Carlisle in 1944-45. Back row: 1st left, Jack Wilson and 1st right, Leonard Patterson. Front row: 1st, Paddy Finnigan, 3rd, Glynn Morgan (captain) from Hazelwood Avenue and 4th, Paddy Moran.

The same RAF Corps as above in 1945 stationed in Egypt. This group of RAFs were unwinding after a few bottles of beer, having a sing song. The tool box is carried by Glynn Morgan.

A group of young people raising funds a youth project in 1995. They cycled from Newlyn Crescent to St Mary's Island and back. From left: Councillor Margaret Nolan, who started the race, James and brother Darren Taws, Michelle Lowry, Norman Mains, unknown, Alan ?, unknown, Mark Ferguson and Wayne Carr.

Ralph Gardner Secondary Modern School's Sports Day in 1958. The girl on the left, front is Christine Morgan, from Hazelwood Avenue.

The Meadow Well Dragoons on Collingwood Field, once the old reservoir site, in the latter part of the 1970s. Many Jazz Bands came far and wide to be at the gathering and to compete with other bands. It was a good day out with the family.

Three members of one of the first ever Jazz Bands on the estate. They were the Meadow Well Oranges and Lemons. The three little girls dressed in their uniform in September 1974 are: Jane Shannon, Tracy Dunning and unknown. One dear lady sat and crochet their ponchos, to keep them warm through the chilly weekend days.

A session with the children at The Meadows, on Waterville Road in 1995. The sessional worker is Hengameh Nazemi ('H'). One of the young girls is Kayleigh Richardson.

Children enjoying the Bouncy Castle at The Meadows Community Centre's Fun Day, around 1996-97. The children include: Kayleigh Steward, her brothers Clifford and Paul and George Watson.

Four of the boys from the Meadow Well enjoying a day out at Holywell Dene in 1991. From left: Paul Johnson, Robert Williamson (Skinny Willy), James Bromwell and Dennis Lemon.

A local girl Ethel Taylor Nathan from Silkey's Lane entered this photograph in a beauty competition in the early 1950s. She was one of three girls who was lucky to be entered in the Top Town Television Competition in Tynemouth in 1953.

EVENTS AND OCCASIONS

Outside their home in Cedarwood Avenue, William Walker and Mary Thompson who were married earlier at Holy Saviour's Church in 1948. The best man A. Greve is on left, Ellen Wright, Wilhemina Nichols and Lily Gibson were bridesmaids.

Winnie Watson and her sister Janet, outside their home in 1935. It was Winnie's wedding day. She married Robert William Brown. The Watson family was one of the first families to make a home on the estate.

The marriage of Glinn Morgan and Margaret Sangster at Christ Church, North Shields in September 1944. Her wedding gown was made from parachute silk. They moved to Hazelwood Avenue after the wedding. Margaret was from Howard Street in North Shields and Glinn's home was in South Wales. They met while both were serving at RAF Crosby and Eden in Carlisle during the war.

The marriage of Grace Rippeth and Thomas Henry (Harry) Nathan on Boxing Day in 1952, on West Percy Road. From left to right: Joseph Rippeth, Norman (Kidder) Murray, Grace and Harry Nathan, Anne Thompson from Woodlea Crescent, Ethel Taylor Nathan and Thomas Nathan, all who lived on the estate.

The marriage of Martha Robinson Rippeth and Brian Wallis took place at the Ridges Methodist Mission in 1959. Here they are standing on the corner of Linden Road and Waterville Road. In 1949 the Mayor, Alderman Richard Irvin JP, accepted the invitation to lay the foundation stone for the premises of the new Mission Hall and Sunday School of Ridges Methodist Mission. As the years passed, membership started to fall. It reduced to less than a dozen or so, and it was impossible to keep the church in operation any longer. The premises closed in May 1969.

Below: The bridesmaids for the marriage of Martha Rippeth and Brian Wallis, outside the Ridges Methodist Mission in 1959. From left: Annie Redhead Rippeth and her sister, Elizabeth Foster Rippeth with Jean Wallis. The child standing in front is Karen Rippeth.

The marriage of George Bean and Jean Brown outside St Peter's Church, on the Balkwell Estate in 1959. Mrs Elizabeth Bean is on George's right and Mrs Winnie Brown on Jean's left.

Right: The marriage of Elizabeth Foster Rippeth and Kenneth Amis took place at the Ridges Methodist Mission in 1964. Ken was from Silkeys Lane and Betty, from Elmwood Road. The estate in 1964 had grown. Shops filled Marina Avenue and Bridge Road South. There were bakers, butchers, grocers, green-grocers, confectioners, newsagents, haberdashers and many more. Smith's Park and the allotments were pastimes for all the family.

A group of bridesmaids for the marriage of Harriot Bean and Alan Overton, a soldier from the Grenadier Guards, outside St John's Church, Percy Main in 1965. Front row: Susan Carol Bean, Susan Bean, Carol Richie and Christine Craig. Back row: Joan Bell, Susan Richie and Anne Bell. St Joseph's Church is the Parish for Percy Main and Meadow Well. A new vicarage was completed in Percy Main in 1955 and the original building was sold and renovated into a public house, The Redburn Inn, to William Younger and Company Limited. Reverend John Clucas moved to the newly built vicarage. He had been serving the community from 1920. He retired in October 1958, at the age of 79 years.

The marriage of George Bean and Jean Brown, outside St Peter's Church in 1959. The bridesmaids were dressed in pale colours, representing a rainbow wedding.

In August 1967, Bernard and Irene Barker, with their children baby Sharon, Annette and John, were guests at a friend's wedding at St Peter's Church.

Leanne Pentz, daughter to Norman and Tanya Pentz, married Andrew Coulton, at the Registry Office in Howard Street, North Shields in June 2000. There was a marvellous view of the quay and the River Tyne from the Registry Office. Here on Ripley Avenue is Leanne, father Norman and bridesmaid Kimberley Rickerby.

First Communion for Hylton Wark and Tina Escrit who both live on the estate. They stand outside St Joseph's School on Wallsend Road in 1992

Below: Members of Hylton's family after the service. Back row: Claire Wark (sister to Hylton), Hylton Wark (father), Anthony Nolan (uncle), Marie Nolan (auntie), and Carol Wark (mother). Front: Hylton Wark, Margaret Nolan (nana) and Mary Baker (great auntie). Behind them is The Pineapple. The Trade Directories of 1786, shows The Pineapple was standing at that time with John Dobson being the landlord and also market gardener. In December 1787, the Dobson family had a son named John who grew up and became a famous architect. He designed the Presbyterian Church, Baptist Chapel in North Shields. He designed Collingwood's Monument overlooking the River Tyne in Tynemouth as well as many well known buildings on Tyneside.

Outside St Joseph's Church in 1970, George and Jean Bean with their daughter Susan at Holy Communion. At St Joseph's Church's opening ceremony in August 1955, Major P. Grant paid tribute to the Faith, Courage and Tireless. 'From now on, let this church be the centre of your Catholic Faith.' He was one of the procession who entered the church for High Mass, with many of the faithful servants of God following.

Below: The Victory Tea Party was held on Waterville Road on the 16th May 1945. Parties such as these were a major event on the estate.

The Victory Tea Party was held on Peartree Crescent on Wednesday, 16th May 1945. Una Rippeth is standing 4th from the right with Richard in her arms. Many of the children only knew their fathers as a man in a photograph. The women

who waited for their menfolk to return had changed. They had independence and equality. Life for the post-war veterans were never the same. Before the war, they rarely ventured out more than fifty miles from the community.

Oakwood Avenue party on the 5th January 1956. The party was held at St Peter's Church Hall in the Balkwell Estate. Only a few names are known: Ann or Sandra Jenson, Doreen and Murial Robb, Peter Moses, Elizabeth (Betty) Bean and Alice Moses. The lady at the window is Mrs Sanderson.

Whitley Bay Girls' Choir in 1954. The young ladies met at a Church Hall in Whitley Bay for choir practice. The photograph was taken at the ladies' dress rehearsal. Second row, 6th from right is, Jean Brown, who lived at Laburnum Avenue.

Chirton Social Club in the mid 1960s. They sit relaxed, supping their pints of ale. From left: Joe Amos, Dick Snowdon, Jimmy Caush, Brian Reynolds, Paddy Cambridge, George Bilton, Florrie Nichols, Ena Bilton, Jimmy Ruddy, Jean Ruddy, Hannah Mealia and Charlie James. Before 1955 the club had a concert room, entertainment from a piano, go as you please and the occasional concert party. In 1955, the first major alterations were made to the club, at the cost of £22,000, providing a sixty seat lounge, a new bar and concert room, with a stage and dressing room facilities.

Ridges Methodist Mission in 1949. His Worship the Mayor of Tynemouth, Alderman Richard Irvin JP, laid the foundation stone for the Mission. Courtesy of North Tyneside Library, this picture was taken from *Romance of the Ridges Methodist Mission* by F. Austin Merrick.

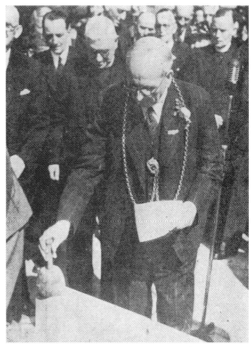

Below: A street party on Wincanton Place in July 1981 celebrating the marriage of Lady Diana Spencer and Prince Charles. Included are: Dale Robson, Denise Lemon (the woman in the hat), Mrs Errington, Lisa Robson, Sonya Lemon with her brother Gary in her arms, Tracy Stagg, David Smith, Michael Robson, Rachel Jones and her sister Beverley.

On Cedarwood Avenue the residents held a street party to celebrate the Queen's Silver Jubilee in June 1977. It was not until 1980 when the Cedarwood Avenue Centre opened nearby.

The official opening of the downstairs of the Cedarwood Trust was held on 20th December 1999. The drop-in centre was once the old children's library on Avon Avenue. It is now part of the Cedarwood Trust. From right: Reverend David Peel, Mrs Molly Woodhouse, behind her, Mrs Ellen Heads and Mick Thompson.

David Hope's 7th birthday party, inside his home on West Percy Road in 1983. From the expression on his face he seems proud and is enjoying his party. Amanda Nathan is sitting next to him. The cups on the table are the commemorative cups of the Prince and Princess of Wales – Charles and Diane.

Britain in Bloom Competition around 1976. Various schools from North Tyneside met to collect their awards. The Mayor of North Tyneside and his wife and Deputy Mayor and Mayoress were there to celebrate with the children. Maxenne Ball (who lives on the estate) stands in the middle with a polo-neck sweater on.

The pensioners' Christmas party at the Collingwood Youth Club on Waterville Road. Included are: Mrs Adams, Sadie ? , Amy ? , Mrs Hilda Gardner, Mrs Lizzie Leck, Mrs Crow, Sarah ? , Miss Woodhouse, Mrs Craig, Mrs Emily Kenny, Mrs Bell McVay, Mrs Annie Bell, Mrs Iris Kyle, Mrs Meggie O'Brian, Mrs Julie Rein and Mrs Meggie Bailey.

Charlene Farelamb's 4th birthday was celebrated in the back garden on Waterville Road in 1992. A few are named. From right: Toni Hillman, her mother Tricia Hillman and baby Dannii. Standing in the middle, Patrick Mason, and on the left of him, Mrs Irene Porter. 1992 was a sad year for the whole estate. They were coming to grips with plans to regenerate parts of the estate after the destruction of 1991. The majority of houses were demolished on the south side; the north side lost the middle area of buildings and the whole area of the westside of the estate also went.

The Reverend David Peel's leaving party at St John's Church in Percy Main in 1987. A few names were put to the folk: William Belfon, Ann Edgar, Sheila Auld, Ann Porter, Donna Spellman, Denise Riach, Brenda Belfon, Carol Wark, Olive Fothergill, Lesley-Ann ?.

A petition was put forward to get David Peel back. He returned in June 1991. David, a Pastoral Priest, has served the community for twenty years at Cedarwood Avenue Centre. It closed and was demolished in 1994. The centre was then transferred to 43 Avon Avenue on the north side of the estate, to continue the on-going work, which they had succeeded in carrying on for so many years. In July 1995 the centre changed its name to Cedarwood Trust.

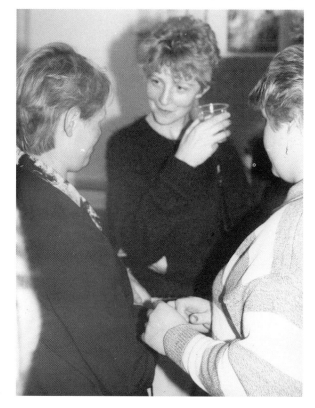

Again at the Reverend David Peel's leaving party. Ann Edgar, Wendy Toby and Margaret Dial enjoying a cup of wine and a friendly chit-chat, surrounded by friends and neighbours who lived on the South Meadow Well Estate.

The litter-pickers were out in force in 1993. The nearby schools met on Collingwood Field on the old reservoir site on Waterville Road. The guest in the middle is actor, Tim Healy. The lady on the left is Mrs Cass. The children were lined up and when Tim Healy honked, off they went to clean their patch of ground for the community.

Avon Avenue in 1993-94. The event was the Keep Britain Tidy Campaign. Children from nearby schools took up the challenge to clean up the estate. Many changes were on their way: the renovations on the homes in Bridge Road South and Ripley Avenue; the foundations of the community centre; the Neighbourhood and Childcare Centre, were only a few out of many changes.

Avon Avenue in 1994. Again this was the Keep Britain Tidy Campaign. Behind the children is Tonbridge Avenue. The Council demolished the street; with Prestbury Avenue, Richmond Grove, Oakwood Gardens, one side of Dorkin Avenue, Compton Road and Newlyn Crescent, and the land sold to the British Housing Association.

The children from Percy Main School in Bedford Street, North Shields in 1993 with their rewards. Prizes were handed out such as: t-shirts, McDonalds' Happy Meals and many more. They volunteered to pick up the litter around the area, while Metro Radio entertained the shoppers. Kevin the Badger was there to help. Many of these children live on the estate. Only a few names are known: Vicky Riley, Chris Fairley, Ryan Ball, Melissa Dixon, Brian Dodds, Elaine Graham, Kirsty Thompson, Steve Cramin, Dean Riley, Ken Robson, Micky Gribbon and Lindsay Thompson.

A group of litter-pickers from the estate, inside McDonalds around 1995-1996, waiting for their well-deserved reward; A McDonalds' Happy Meal. A few of the children are known: Kenneth Robson, Chris Fairley, Ian Maholane, Willy New, Dean Riley, Scott Hamilton, Micky Farman, Steve King, Michael Dodds and Michael Grant.

A Fun Day event was held on Collingwood Field in the early 1990s. Courtesy from Rington's Tea for the use of a traditional horse and cart. The boy sitting in the middle of the cart is Lee Crow. The boy on the bike is William Anderson. The young girl leading the horse and cart is Leanne Pederson.

A number of children from Waterville Primary School going on a school trip around 1992. A few of the children are known: Laura Cramin, Billy Anderson and Tony Whitelaw.

A class from Waterville Primary School. They are on a school trip to Byker Farm.

In 1995-1996 a group of children from nearby homes pose for the camera for the Child Safety Week. They are at the rear-end of the Meadow Well Community Centre. The building at the right, was built by the Meadow Well Construction Company, for their own business. The children are: Michael Grant, Daniella Williamson, Kayleigh Richardson, Amy and Katie McVie, Mikey Pederson, Lindsay Graham, Lee Crow, Craig Graham, Hylton Wark David Wark and Paul Whiting. The two workers are Alison Williamson and Carol Wark.

Collingwood Youth Club on Waterville Road in 1990. A meeting held by the Housing Action Group to stop North Tyneside Council from selling and demolishing the houses on the estate to private builders. Denise Riach and Val Mianro were two who chaired the meeting. Many residents attended the meeting as they were concerned about their own homes. The club was a major centre point for the people. Children and adults gathered there for activities, as well as news or prospects concerning the people who live in the surrounding area.

A few of the residents left the estate to attend the Poll Tax March in London in 1990. From right: Raymond Reynolds, Edward Farquhar, Ann Porter, Ann Bishop, Councillor Margaret Nolan, Colin Penrith, Nancy Peters and sitting down is Ethel Longstaff.

A demonstration was held outside the Co-op supermarket on Waterville Terrace, North Shields in 1990. The demonstration was to save the Meadow Well Community Right's Centre, situated on the corner of Ripley Avenue and Avon Avenue. The Community Rights Centre was similar to today's Citizens Advice Bureau.

In 1989, the Meadow Well Action Group arrived in Leeds and demonstrated against the selling of the estate's homes. Only a few names are known: Ann Bishop and her two children, Trevor and Lisa Bishop, Ann Porter, Barry ? Bobby Day, Margaret Nolan and Edward Farquhar.

In 1988, a residents' meeting was held at Ralph Gardner High School on Chirton Green. Councillor David Corkey is the one who is pointing. Quite a few meetings were held here, as Council Officials were forced by Government to reduce schools which were using too much expenditure with the smallest numbers attending. The  Education Department, after consultation with the High Schools of the area, decided Ralph Gardner High School was to close. The school closed, after much fighting to save it, and was demolished in 1994.

The Meadow Well Mini Job Centre was on Collingwood Field, on the old reservoir site, around 1992. The mini bus was given to the Meadow Well Credit Union for the use of all organisations on the estate. Sitting down is Susan Crow with her daughter Jamie. Kerry New is inside the van.

Members of the Credit Union and their families going on holiday to Northumberland in 1987. A few names are known: Edward Farquhar, Trevor Bishop, his sister Lisa and mother Ann, Louise Porter and her mother Ann and Dean Riley

The opening ceremony at the new Community Centre in October 1994. Visitors attended with officials and members of the media. Later in the afternoon, Alan Robson and Metro Radio parked across Waterville Road and entertained the children and adults alike. A few are known: Kath Thompson, Dennis Marsh, Jill Allen, Keeks McGarry, Joseph Marsh, Pauline Wright and Stephen Byers MP. The children: Mark King, Darren Richardson and Shauna Longstaff.

The estate had a visit from officials who displayed, for the media, the CCTV cameras on Waterville Road on the 4th October 1996. The officials were Neville Trotter, MP for Tynemouth and Home Secretary Michael Howard. They were surrounded by police and minders.

In April 1995, the Seine Boat on Waterville Road had a sponsored event of five-a-side football. Men played against women in fancy dress.

The winners of an Art Competition in 1994. The design was for the new Metro Station on the estate. The event was held at the Neighbourhood and Childcare Centre. Two children are known: Dean Riley (3rd left) and Steven Stonebanks (5th left). Two adults are known: Councillor Margaret Nolan (6th left) and Carol Bell (7th left).

The Meadow Well Garden Competition in 1999. These are the winners for best-kept gardens on the estate. A few of the names are: Moira Partridge, Ann Brown, Ellen Heads, Jean Gilgallon, David Hall, Gordon White and Mr Frazer.

St John's Church Hall in Percy Main, 1981-82. Back row: Nancy Hunter, unknown, Mrs Adams, Reverend Stephen Huxley, June Parry, Ena Reeves and unknown. Front row, first two on left: Josie Oskarsen and Marion Errington. The remainder are not known. Reverend Stephen Scott Huxley held the Parish of Percy Main and Meadow Well from the 9th September 1978. He held morning assembly at Percy Main and Percy St John's Schools. The curate in 1979 was David Charles Peel, who became Project Leader for Cedarwood Avenue Centre on 8th September 1980. Reverend Huxley retired on the 22nd February 1987 and Reverend John Michael Pennington MA held the position of vicar for the Parish.

Cedarwood Trust's Women's Writing Group reads poetry from their own inspiration at the MetroCentre in Gateshead in 1989. From the left: Sandra Cussins, Denise New, Ann Edgar, Annette Smith, Linda Graham and Sheila Auld.

Cedarwood Trust's Women's Writing Group entertained a few guests from the Iona Community, at Horsham Grove Centre in 1990-91. Back row, from left: Sheila Auld, Edna Allen, Ann Robinson, Mary Cussins, Brenda Belfon, Carol Wark and Margaret Turner. Front row: Joanne Belfon, Karen Graham, Denise Dodds, Jan Duffin, Linda Graham and Denise Dodds. Sheila Auld became Deacon in 1994 and was ordained Priest in July 1995. She works as a Pastoral Priest and Project Worker for Cedarwood Trust.

In October 1999 Cameron Hope's 8th birthday party, held on Ripley Avenue with a few of his friends. From left: Jason Pocklington, James Gilgallon, hiding behind James is his guardian, Dave Hall, Dale Blythe, Martin Stevens and Cameron Hope. The game they are playing is called 'Statues' – a game where the children dance and when the music stops, the children must keep perfectly still, if not, they are out. The child who is left on the floor alone is the winner.

A few of the local lasses gathered in the dining room on Ripley Avenue away from the men, Christmas 1999. They enjoyed the last Christmas before the Millennium. From left: Charlotte Haines, Amanda Nathan, Victoria Storey and Jennifer Haines.

The dedication of the Memorial Garden on the old reservoir site on 2nd September 2000. These three men are important to our estate. From left: Reverend David Peel, Pastoral Priest and Project leader for the Cedarwood Trust, Reverend Charles Hope, Parish Priest for Percy Main and Meadow Well and Canon Alec Barrass, Roman Catholic and Parish Priest for Chirton and Meadow Well.

On the 2nd September 2000 at the dedication of the Memorial Garden on the day of the Millennium Celebrations at The Meadows. From left: Dawn Heads, Reverend David Peel, Canon Alec Barrass and Aidan Doyle. Dawn opened the service with a few words written by Ellen Heads (she was unable to attend). Reverend David Peel and Canon Alec Barrass said prayers for those who are no longer with us. The Memorial Garden is to be used for quiet thought. Only white flowers are allowed to be planted on this site. Aidan Doyle created and planted the garden, with the help of a few of the nearby children, his friend Viv and Nora Brunton. Shortage of money has stopped the development and the rest of the field can not be completed.

A local group, 'Gangsters of Ska', performed at The Meadows for the Millennium Celebrations in September 2000. From left: J.T. Snake (bass guitarist), Ian O'B (singer), T.A. Alfie (drums), Blind Art (organist) and the Fat Controller (saxophone).

On the 2nd September 2000, the day of the Millennium Celebrations at The Meadows on Waterville Road. Willy Laidler, the Lord's Town Crier, walked round the estate with his bell and informed the people of the celebrations with his cry.

SECTION FIVE

SCHOOLDAYS

North Shields Nursery School on Howdon Road in 1936. There was a special visit to the nursery from the Right Honourable Lord Eustace Percy MP and His Worship the Mayor of Tynemouth, Alderman A.L. Armstrong JP. The superintendent was Miss Hilda Davidson. Lady Astor opened the Nursery to the children in April 1934. It held 40 children, between the ages of 2 to 5 years. Parents paid what they could afford towards the cost of meals. Three meals a day would cost 2 shillings a week per child. Miss Davidson was assisted by a paid cook, a probationer and voluntary helpers. A rota of volunteers was formed and two were in attendance every day. The Square Building Trust founded the site on Howdon Road.

North Shields Nursery School on Howdon Road in 1934. The building had a large airy playroom with windows on three sides, opening on to a covered veranda on the south-east side. The bathroom had wash basins, supplying hot and cold water and fixed to a correct height, so that the children  could wash themselves. A small bath was placed at a height to make it easy for the attendants to bathe the children. Every child had their own towel hung on its own peg, comb, toothbrush and mug all at easy reach for the child. Small WC's were screened off but low enough to allow supervision. A cloakroom, medical and staff rooms were provided. The nursery had a drying room, bed and blanket stores. A kitchen was equipped for the preparation of meals and used also as a staff dining room. The building was erected with good timber-built structure and supplied with central heating. The estimated cost of the Nursery was £1,000.

Western Board School in 1949. Between 1945 to 1951, the headmaster was M.M. Sinclair. The school was situated on Burdon Main Row and opened its doors to 172 boys in May 1874, with a weekly fee of one penny. The headmaster was John Mavor. In 1914 the girls joined the school, in another part of the building, and the headteacher was U. Pybus.

Ralph Gardner School near Chirton Green in 1935. The school was opened to staff and pupils on the 3rd June 1935 and replaced the Royal Jubilee School. Yet, the opening ceremony was on the 5th June, and performed by Deputy Mayor Councillor A. Norman Parks and Alderman J.W. Fitzhugh OBE, Chairman of Tynemouth Education Committee. Many respected officials were also present. The headteachers were Mr Duncan Snowdon and Miss Florence Bell. Both heads fulfilled their appointments until 1947 and 1944 respectively. The school held 960 pupils in 1935, taking the youngest age of 11 years from various schools. The estimated cost of the school was £46,860 and the contract was let to Alexander Anderson of Newcastle-upon-Tyne.

A class at the Percy St John's School before the First World War. These children can not be named, except for one. A mother who has gone, but is not forgotten – Olive May Gardner (from right, 1st on second last row).

Western Board School in the late 1940s. A class of boys outside a stone-walled school. Front row: Brian Grant, Ronnie Stonebanks, unknown, ? Nesbitt, Brian Colesby, Thomas Wright, unknown, unknown and ? Gillespie. Second row: 1st, Brian Dunn. Back row: 4th, Roy Curry, 5th, Dave ? , 6th, Joseph Blacklock and 8th, George Craven. Mr J.P. Haswell was responsible for the design of the school in 1872. He designed Christ Church School in Norfolk Street in 1870 and Tynemouth Infirmary in Hawkey's Lane in 1889 and many more. The school amalgamated and became a mixed school in 1954, with the head teacher D. Brodrick.

Right: A class at the Ridges Council School in 1949-1950. Back row, middle: Robin Nathan. Front row: 1st left, Annie Redhead Rippeth. The school was brought about by the development of the Ridges Estate and the slum clearance operations from the Fish Quay Bankside. The contract was given to the sub-contractors Messrs J.R. Rutherford and Sons Limited from Newcastle-upon-Tyne. The final cost of the erection of the building was £17,565 12s 1d, with Architect's fees, Quantity Surveyor and legal expenses included.

A class at the Ridges Infant School in 1948-1949. Three children are named: Front row, right: 1st, Elizabeth Foster Rippeth and 6th Annie Redhead Rippeth. Back row, right: 6th, Robin Nathan. The site of the school was one of the best in the town and off the main traffic route. The classrooms were on the southside of the building, giving the children ideal conditions with all sunshine possible. It had 'closed corridors' which they could open for fresh air when required. The school was to accommodate no more than 450 children, aged five and over, who lived anywhere on the estate.

Miss McCormick's class in 1949 at St Joseph's Primary School. Back row: Joan Stonebanks, Julia Suniga, Maureen Barron, Majorie Hingston, Betty Moses, Lillian Flaherty, Hazel Morton, Betty Bean, Murial Parsons, Margaret Ferguson and Mary Bell. Third row: Brian Jennings, Robert Knowles, George Aylett, Earnest Anderson, Billy McGee, Andrew Murphy, John Office, Cuthbert Burn, John Ridland, Kenneth Thompson and Ronnie Burns. Second row: Ann Laidlaw, Maureen Costello, Sarah O'Dowd, Joan Andrews, Ann Towell, Joan Tait, Lavinia Joyce, Eleanor Ray, Olive Mavin, Pat Conaty, Dolores Guillan and Brenda Villaverds. Front row: Billy Welsh, John Mulgrove, Alan Flannigan, George Horseborough, Victor Blacklock, Terry Thompson, Gerrard Latimer and Arthur Chater.

Ralph Gardner Secondary Modern School in 1951. Third year boys pose outside the school. Only three boys are known. Back row, from left: John Henderson (3rd) and Eddie Millsip (4th). Middle row, 6th left: Dennis Lawson. On the 1st October 1947, the foundation stone was laid for the extension building on the west-side of the school, by Alderman G. Forsyth, Chairman of Tynemouth Education Committee. The extension was carried out in three phases. The first of which was to provide five new classrooms and offices. The second phase was to add another classroom and a library and finally, two gymnasiums were built. The assembly halls were enlarged and two dining rooms with kitchens provided. The new extension of the school was officially opened on the 18th April 1951, by Councillor W.R. Forster, Chairman of Tynemouth Education Committee.

Western Board School in 1951. The pupils were in their last year at the school and many of them or all, would go on to the nearby school, Ralph Gardner. Back row, from left: Sylvia Stoneman, Ellen Wright, Dorothy Tait, Margaret Hewitson, Pat

Cauley, Margaret Wilson and Elizabeth Wilson. Middle row: Beatrice George, Rita Henderson, Lilian Hardy, Margaret Vasse, Thelma Weeks, Hazel Woods and Margaret Rowley. Front row: unknown, Margaret Crossland, Doreen Wells, Carol Coin, Nancy Tait, June McClarion, Maureen Maniham, Joyce Chambers and Rita ?. In March 1951, the headteacher was M.M. Sinclair. Yet, in the same year, the post of head was given to H.M. Stewart.

Year 2, St Cuthbert's School in 1953. The school was celebrating Empire Day. Front row: Ann Wall, Thelma Johnson, Maureen Laidler, unknown, Joan Andrews, unknown, Dorothy Hall and Sylvia Smith. Middle row: 4th from left, Pauline Commerford. Back row: 4th, ? Gillespie, Betty Bean and Florence Walsh.

St Joseph's Roman Catholic Primary School on Wallsend Road in 1960. The foundation stone for the school was laid by Bishop McCormack in February 1939, and led by the Hebburn Catholic Fife and Drum Band. The school officially opened on the 28th August 1939. The first session had 312 children present. Mr W. Skelly was headmaster and there were nine members of staff. The number on roll at the end of the week was 331 pupils attending the school. The school had seven classrooms, an infant assembly hall and staff rooms were joined to the existing Parish Hall, which was to be used as an assembly hall when necessary. Gardens surrounded the school.

Ridges Council School in 1962-1963. Back row: 3rd, Dave Henderson, 6th, Audrey Amin and 7th, John Ferguson. Third row: 2nd, Brenda Robson, 4th, Jennifer Lewis, 5th, Jeffrey Lewis, 7th, Ian Burn and 8th, John Toes. Front row: 2nd, Clive Whiting, 3rd, ? Blakey, 5th, Alan Sutherland and 6th, Phillip Henderson.

Western Board School in 1965. A class of 7 and 8 year olds, outside the school. The headteacher was D. Brodrick. Back row: unknown, Raymond Reynolds, Richard Smith, unknown, Linda Hamilton, Steven Turner, David Sunderland, Jean Beanshill, Christine Foggit, Catherine Strong and unknown. Middle row: Brenda Horseborough, Colin Campbell, Christopher Casey, Maureen Templeton, David Churnside, Tony Giandrea, Joan Chambers, Wendy Craig, Shaun Longstaff, Brian ? and Michael Walker. Front row: Yvonne Hooks, Ann Elgie, Jean Culyer, Judith Mattison, Linda Abdullah, unknown, unknown, Jacqueline Roper, Anna Marriott and unknown.

Year 2b at Ralph Gardner Secondary Modern School in 1967. Back row: Ann Turnbull, Marion Mckelvie, unknown, unknown, Maureen Agnew, unknown, Sheila Leslie, Linda ? and Miriam ?. Middle row: Christine McLocklin, unknown, Catherine O'Donnell, unknown, Diane ?, Sharon ?, Linda Nathan, Brenda Wilson and unknown. Front row: Jean Horseborough, Jean Wilson, Jean MacDonald, Linda Cass, Mrs Hopkins (teacher), Susan Smith, Christine Office, unknown and Gillian Phillips.

This photograph was taken in 1966 at Ralph Gardner Secondary Modern School. Class 2b, Miss Moony was the class teacher. Needlework was her subject. Back row, from left: Margaret Foreman, Margaret Brown, Janet McQuire, Elizabeth Boak, Lynn Chapman, Jennifer Nelson, Patricia Campbell and Susan Compson. Middle row: Valerie Carr, Hazel Waite, Shelagh Bracken, Ester Kelly, unknown, unknown, Margaret Horseborough, Sandra Greenwood, Eileen Hair and Elaine Maine. Front row: Linda Slaughter, unknown, Joan Heslop, unknown, Patricia Nathan, Miss Moony(teacher), Margaret Johnson, Hazel Croft, Majorie Young, Margaret Wilson and Norma Thompson.

Ralph Gardner Secondary Modern School, fourth year, in 1967. Back row: Margaret Darby, Linda Gardner, Karen Hopkins, Linda Farmen, Valerie Lannon (Blacklock), Jaqueline Ridsdale, Anne Smith, Florence Duel, Avril O'Sullivan, Ann Greeley and Joan Bowman. Front row: Christine Kaye, Maureen Thirkell, Cynthia Barrass, Doreen Ishamor, Miss Laverick (teacher), unknown, Susan ?, Irene Verte and Heather Reed.

Ralph Gardner High School in 1976. These pupils were in their last year. Only three names are known, back row, left: 4th, James Heads, 5th, Brian Dolton and 7th, Graham Thompson. From 1967 to 1973 changes were carried out to combine both boys and girls, without distruption. Boys were asked to join cookery, needlework and art lessons with the girls, and girls were asked to join wood and metal work with the boys. Many were apprehensive at first. Miss Ord the headmistress, who replaced Miss Rochester in 1959, retired in 1969. Mr Brassington became headmaster for both schools, as they amalgamated in September of that year and Ralph Gardner Secondary Modern became, Ralph Gardner High School, also in 1969.

Year 4b at Ralph Gardner Secondary Modern School in 1969. Back row: Shiela Leslie, Carol Stevenson, Marion Mckelvie, Brenda Wilson, Linda Hamilton, Linda Errington and Jean Horseborough. Middle row: unknown, Linda Nathan, unknown, unknown, Catherine O'Donnell, Diane ?, unknown and Maureen Agnew. Front row: Lynn Barren, unknown, Susan Smith, unknown, Mrs Richardson (teacher), Sharon ?, Gillian Phillips, Susan Wilson and Jean Wilson.

The prefects and headmistress, Miss Ord at Ralph Gardner Secondary Modern School in 1969, taken inside the gym hall. The final term for Miss Ord and for a few of the pupils. At the end of the summer holidays, the school had been renovated and boys and girls were mixed, altering its standards and becoming Ralph Gardner High School. Only a few are known. Back row, left: 4th, Susan Compton and 10th, Susan Wilson. Middle row: 8th, Shelagh Bracken and 9th, Patricia Nathan. Front row: 2nd, Majorie Young.

Early 1970-1971, Queen Victoria School had a pantomime. The children were dressed up as sailors for 'The Sailor's Hornpipe Dance'. Only a few names are known. Back row, left: ? Blythe, 3rd, Jeffrey Stevenson and 4th, ? Webb. Front row: 5th, David Heads.

The pantomime 'Batman and the Butter Mountain' at Ralph Gardner High School in 1989. Ralph Gardner declined in numbers of pupils who attended the school. Council Officials began looking through the Borough of Tynemouth at all the oldest schools. After consultation they closed the school. School Governors and parents opting out of Council control and to become a Grant Maintained by the Government, yet this was not to be, the Council strongly opposed it. In October 1993, the application for grant-maintained status was rejected and the Council announced the closure of the school immediately.

In 1989, Ralph Gardner High School was showing a pantomime. Councillor David Corkey was in an American Highway Patrol uniform. The pantomime was all about the mountains of butter stored away, which no-one could get their hands on.

Right: A few of the actors from 'Batman and the Butter Mountain' taking time out in the dressing room. Councillor David Corkey dressed in a Highway Patrol uniform and Denise Riach standing in the background.

A Pantomime performed by the children at Western Primary School in 1982-1983. 2nd on left: Lisa Cohone.

A Pantomime performed by the children at Western Primary School around 1983. Two of the girls are known. Front row, 2nd from left: Michelle Wilson. Back row, 5th from left: Suzie Malvern.

Percy St John's School in 1994-1995. The children were waiting to go out and collect the litter for People and Places, an organisation which began in the early 1990s with Carol Bell in charge of the operation. Only a few are known: Rachel Chambers, Chris Grey, John Paul Johnson and Louise Armstrong.

'Joseph and His Amazing Technicolour Dream Coat' performed by the children at Waterville Primary School in 1999. Only a few names are known on this photograph. Included are: Kelly Campbell, Katie Wenn, Lindsay Farelamb, Cheryl Beanshill, Lindsey Strong, Katie Charlton, Charlotte Mason and Craig Scott.

Waterville School is in the middle of construction. One part of the school has been pulled down and building started on a section of the new school. On completion, the builders will demolish the remainder of the old school and build the other part, without any disruption to the children's lessons. They are hoping to be completed by 2001.

Waterville Primary School, Easter Bonnet Parade in 1998. The children are parading their creations and brilliant ideas.

A Nativity Play performed by the children at Waterville Primary School in 1998. In 1994 the school was officially re-named Waterville Primary School, with Mrs M. Duncan as headmistress.

The end of term club at Waterville Primary School in 1998. The children are dressed in rabbit costumes. The club runs various after school hours activities.

Choir practice at Waterville Primary School in 1998. The girls are, from left: Charlotte Haines, Samantha Culyer and Maria Armstrong. Behind the girls are: Anthony Storey and Leanne Hayes. Choir practice is held every week, where the pupils can display their own music talents.

A pantomime 'Oliver Twist' performed by the children at Waterville Primary School. The school has a variety of pantomimes every year and it takes much of the teachers and pupils time up. However, the pupil experience stardom, helping them to read, to remember and express their own personalities.

Another scene from 'Oliver Twist' performed by the children at Western Primary School in the 1980s.

A Christmas party for the children at Western Primary School in the early 1990s. The pantomimes and parties the school have are so close together that the young children realise that Christmas is almost upon them, because Santa is coming and its the end of term.

A litter-picking day for the pupils at Ralph Gardner High School in 1994. It was the last time this event happened. The school closed in July 1994, never to open again. Mr Neil McCleod, headmaster since 1981 had a message for the pupils. 'Life must go on. A school is not a building, a school is about people who have memories and with these memories schools can't die.' He went on to say, 'I set myself three tasks; one, was to get my children settled into other schools. My second, was to make sure that my excellent colleagues did not go to waste and my third, was to see that the school's equipment, books and records were found a good home, all of which I have accomplished.' Demolition was completed at the end of October 1994.

Ralph Gardner High School in 1994. The removal van outside the school is removing the school's memorabilia. It finally closed a few weeks later and demolished soon after. No trace of the school could be found in 1995. The land was sold and the erection of houses had started. The area when completed was named Gardner Park.

Waterville Primary School in 1997. The school's original name was Western Board School. In the Year 2000, half the school has been pulled down to make room for a new school. This way, very little disruption was made to the children's lessons.

Meadow Well Primary School in 1997. The school's original name was the Ridges Day School. From 1994 Mrs M. MacDonald has been employed as headmistress for the school. Prior to her was Miss Jean Howard. The school has three divisions, infant, junior and nursery pupils. The school held 168 pupils, aged from 3-11 years in 1996. In each classroom there is a computer for the use of the children of all ages, including the nursery pupils.

St Joseph's Roman Catholic Primary School. The photograph was taken in 1997. In 1989, St Joseph's School celebrated their Golden Jubilee. Teaching methods have changed since they began in August 1939, with a lot of parent involvement, which was not present then. Good teaching standards have been maintained in the school with excellent progress.

North Shields Nursery School in 1995. In 1983 the nursery was closed down. The children and staff were transferred to a new nursery, within Percy St John's School, with Miss Parson as headmistress and Miss Watts assisting her. The old nursery on Howdon Road, built of wood, was condemned as a fire hazard. Demolition was inevitable. Thirteen years later in 1996, the threats of closure to the nursery and school came once again. Through Government cuts the closure took place in July 1997.

We end this chapter on schools with this photograph with many familiar faces. Miss McLean's class at St Joseph's Primary School in 1950. Back row: Earnest Anderson, Robert Knowles, John Ridland, Victor Blacklock, Joe Saint, George Horseborough, Kenneth Thompson, George Aylett and Andrew Murphy. Third row: Lillian Flaherty, Eleanor Ray, Majorie Hingston, Julia Suniga, Maureen Costello, Mary Bell, Murial Parsons, unknown, Betty Moses, Hazel Morton, Ann Laidlaw and Maureen Barron. Second row: Margaret Ferguson, Betty Bean, Ann Towel, Lavinia Joyce, Joan Stonebanks, Pat Conaty, Joan Andrews, Dolores Guillan, Olive Mavin and Sarah O'Dowd. Front row: Billy McGee, Cuthbert Burn, Billy Welsh, John Office, Terry Thompson, Alan Flannigan, Brian Jennings, Gerrard Larimer, Arthur Chater and John Mulgrove.

PEOPLE

Ethel Taylor Nathan and her sister Marion
Florence, outside their home at Silkey's Lane in
the late 1940s. Their father, Thomas, was a
bricklayer by trade and a keen gardener.
Thomas Nathan and his wife Mary Ethel was
one of the first families to move on the estate.
They lived in Chirton after they were married
and raised five children at Silkey's Lane. For a
time Thomas worked for Tynemouth Council.

Mrs Welsh and her grand daughter, Irene Nichols, outside her home on Briarwood Avenue in the late 1940s. Many changes were happening on the estate at this time, food rationing was still in force after the war. The men came home discharged from their service and found life different. Life for the families whose men did not come home, had to go on. The young men who had missed the war, at the age of eighteen, joined the National Service.

Below: A group of neighbouring children, fascinated by the huge motor bike, on Oakwood Avenue in 1956. They test it out and experience sitting on it for the first time. The children are, from left to right: Russell Jackson, Norman Jackson, Heather Jackson and standing against the fence is Elizabeth (Betty) Bean. The motorbike is a Douglas 500cc.

Standing outside their home on West Percy Road in 1954, Elizabeth Rippeth (Betty) and her sister Anne. The small child next to them is their niece Karen Rippeth. Betty and Anne are twins and they were the second youngest out of a family of nine children. The family moved to West Percy Road in 1939, prior to there, was Elmwood Road. They moved on the estate in 1934, with three children. They lived in Upper Toll Street, not far from the Fish Quay.

Below: Three shy little girls, posing for the camera outside their grandparent's home on West Percy Road in October 1958. From left to right: Karen Rippeth (aged 6), Linda Nathan (aged 4) and Patricia Nathan (aged 5). Hair ribbons were common in those days, nothing like bobbles and clipped slides we have today. Pinafores were suited for children at that age, they had no waist to hold the skirt to.

Standing in the front garden on Pinetree Gardens, in their Easter clothing, on Good Friday, 16th April 1954. They are: Douglas Cook and Maureen Brown. Blazers were quite fashionable in those days, the bigger they were, the more wear they had before the children grew out of them. All the houses on the estate had metal framed windows and wooden garden rails or concrete slabs to border the gardens (back and front).

Cedarwood Avenue, on the south-side of the estate in 1962. A young child, Keith Heads, playing with his favourite toy outside his home. Besides wooden rails, they had wooden latt gates and banisters to support and confine the families in their own environment.

In the front garden of West Percy Road in 1956, two children, Patricia (the tallest) and her sister Linda Nathan, who were visiting their grandparents, Joseph and Grace Rippeth.

In the back garden of West Percy Road around 1941-1942, Richard Rippeth, the smallest child, and Una his sister. Many families on the estate had allotments, to grow their own vegetables to save those few pennies for food and clothing, they usually cannot afford to buy otherwise. The children's father Joseph had an allotment. Besides growing vegetables he grew flowers and kept chickens.

At Christmas time, inside Mr and Mrs Robert Brown's home on Laburnum Avenue in 1958. The two young men are George Bean and Robert Brown Jnr. Christmas on the estate was an exciting time for the children and a worry for the parents. Christmas trees were small and very little decoration around the walls and ceilings. Crepe paper streamers were made and hung. The children, if the families were large, were lucky if they received a hand-made wooden boat or a doll's house; or a doll or teddy bear; a book and an orange. Yet, whatever the children received, they were happy to know that Santa Claus had been and they had not been forgotten.

Left: Friends posing for the camera in 1956. From left: Ivy Harbran, Elsie Cook and Jean Brown, outside Jean's home on Laburnum Avenue.

In 1958, George Bean (left) outside his home on Oakwood Avenue, with his friend, Michael Chapman. These young men joined the craze of Teddy Boys and hit the dance halls with their new trend – bopping. Besides the craze of fashion, music was another trend. Here are a few favourites the young ones enjoyed in the late 1950s: Buddy Holly – *Peggy Sue*, Jerry Lee Lewis – *Great Balls of Fire*, Bill Haley and the Comets – *Rock Around the Clock*, Brenda Lee – *Lets Jump the Broomstick*, Helen Shipero – *Walking Back to Happiness*, Little Richard – *Good Golly Miss Molly*, Eddie Cochran – *Summertime Blues* and Frankie Vaughan – *Green Door*.

A group of friends on Silkey's Lane in 1948-1949. Back row: Thomas Henry (Harry) Nathan, who was serving his National Service, and his friend Walter Dorian. In front are their girlfriends, Margaret Hunt and Ruby Brown. The fashion in the late 1940s were pin-stripped suits for men and women.

Christine (4) and her brother Hayden Morgan (5) at Hazelwood Avenue in 1951.

Mick Nolan standing outside his home on Larkspur Place with his daughter Carol in 1966.

Ethel Taylor Brown, widow, standing outside her home on Silkey's Lane around 1967. Ethel lived in Chirton for many of her younger days when she married Robert Earnest Brown, a pitman. Her family disowned her for marrying a man below her station. Very little is known about her childhood and her parents. They say her family was from Russia and fled to England. Her husband died from a stone fall at Hollywell Pit in 1917. Ethel died in 1968 at the age of 89 years. She lived with her daughter Mary Ethel and her husband Thomas Nathan, when they married in 1930. The dog she holds is Aster, the family pet.

Mary Ethel Nathan, holding her pet poodle, Aster outside her home on Silkey's Lane in 1967. Mary lived at Silkey's Lane from 1934. She brought up five children and her, and her husband, worked for many years. Her mother Ethel Brown lived with them and looked after the home and children. It was not long after, that the estate went through major renovations in 1969. Tenants were moved out and the houses were stripped to a shell.

Outside her mother-in-law's home on Silkey's Lane around 1970, Cathleen Nathan and her three children: Cathleen, Pamela and Kevin. It was not long after that the family moved to Canada. Her husband Robin was an ambitious man, the North East had little to offer him and they began their new life abroad. His parents, Thomas and Mary Nathan, lived in Silkey's Lane, across the road from them. The view outside their home each morning, from 1969, was like a building site from the renovations the estate was going through. Their parents had moved out to live the rest of their lives on Eustace Avenue, near Billy Mill Lane. They were in private flats.

Soaking up the sun on a summer's day, Elizabeth (Betty) Rippeth and her niece, Linda Nathan, sitting on the steps on West Percy Road in 1959.

Outside their home in Woodlea Crescent in 1969, Susan Bean and her baby brother, Steven, playing with the neighbouring children. Renovations were on their way, starting on the north-side of the estate and finishing on the south-side in 1972. The children played happily. Very few cars used the crescent. Children played Hop-Scotch; Jacks; Skips and Rounders in the middle of the road. Many of the children played in Smith's Park where the playground rides like: swings, the banana slide, shuggy-boat, a round-about and the wide open fields for football and rugby; tennis courts and bowling greens were often used. Chirton Dene was next to the park, it ran sparingly to the River Tyne. Trees and sand-stone bridges enhanced the Dene. Further

across were more bowling greens and the allotments. Minton Lane and Howdon Road, bordered the allotments and Smith's Park. Shops on Bridge Road South were plentiful. Every item a mother needed for food was there. The estate in 1969, was full of children. All playing outside, with no worries of strangers or cars. Everyone looked out for the children.

Oakwood Avenue in 1965. From left: Angela Slaughter; Keith Heads and his brother Jimmy, outside their home. The stuffed animal with wheels on, was common for the toddlers, and balls, for boys and girls.

A group of young children, all related, sitting on the steps enjoying an ice lolly on a warm summer's day. Outside Mr & Mrs Robert Hopkins' house on Limewood Road in 1967. Back row: Lynn Brown, Anthony Brown, James Octolonie and Pauline Wallis. Front row: Mark Brown and Gillian Amis.

An angelic group of brother and sisters, who lived on Silkeys Lane in 1973. From left: Melanie, Angela, Kenneth and Gillian Amis. The parents are Ken and Elizabeth Amis. The estate in 1973 had completed its renovations, with wood-framed windows and open-plan fronts. Gardens were at the rear, and the flats were converted into houses, only a few flats remained. The roundabout on Waterville Road was removed.

A group of girls at a children's birthday party on Presbury Road in 1976. Included are: Christopher Nolan, Michelle Johnson, Madeline Brown, Gwen Wark, Anthony Nolan, Sean Curran, Maureen Curran, Theresa Duffy and Joanne Ramshaw.

In the back garden at Rosetree Crescent in 1987, Claire Blacklock and her younger sister Lorna with Michael Hope in the middle of them, all enjoying a game of water fights. The two children on the other side of the fence, eager to join in are Clair and brother Lee McCathy. This is the way many youngsters spent and enjoyed their summer holidays. Rarely, a few of the families went on holiday, most could not afford it. Day trips were organised for only a minority of the families. Their day's outings would be at the coast in Tynemouth Long Sands or the Fish Quay Sands, or the local Smith's Park. A group of mothers brought out their children and played rounders in the middle of the street, always on a warm summer evening. Many families on the south-side of the estate, enclosed their gardens with scrap wood, to confine their privacy away from the neighbours.

In 1982, David Hope's birthday party on West Percy Road. Front: unknown, Amanda Nathan, David Hope and Colin Robinson. Back row: Michael Hope and his sister Sylvia and Melanie Amis.

Below: Sitting inside their daughter's home in Woodlea Crescent in 1981. From left: Thomas Henry (Harry) Nathan with his granddaughter Amanda Nathan sitting on his knee, next to him is his wife Grace and their son Paul, who is spread across the back of the settee.

David Hope, baby Amanda Nathan and the boy's sister Sylvia. Their pet dog is lying between them and all were enjoying the summer's day on West Percy Road in 1981. The north-side of the estate had open-planned streets. Paths led to each house and trees lined the road sides. The houses had central heating, rear gardens and paths. Shops on Avon Avenue were full of wares and too many burglars. The houses were open to every

opportunist thief when the occupants were out, and yet, as I speak about the fears families had, every neighbour was a friend and was always there to help.

Mrs Ellen Head's back garden on Waterville Road in 1994. Her grandchildren, were all lined up for the camera. From left: Trudi and Kayleigh Heads, Jemma Whittle, Debra and Daniel Heads, Anthony Whittle and Kane Heads. In 1994, many changes were happening. Centres and water parks were built and many streets of houses were demolished. The Royal Quays Development was also in progress. Many families were moved off the estate and the folk's attitudes changed. The renovations of houses were underway in 1994. Roads and paths were taken up and relaid. Families were living on a building site at times and when they had completed the street, the next one became the same. The year 2000 has seen the completion of the estate and now, the families must go through a series of internal work in their homes.

The Information Shop on Avon Avenue in 1989. Denise Riach and one of the workers acting the part of an idiot. Denise raised the Housing Action Group off the ground.

Inside their home at Rosetree Crescent in 1987. A whole family together, from left: Peter David Hope, his wife Patricia with Michael and Sylvia next to them. On the floor is David, their youngest. The parents had little cash to keep their families in food and clothing. Borrowing money until their next pay day, a giro drop and missing Peter to pay Paul. That's how most families lived.

April 1995 on Ripley Avenue, from left: Cameron Hope, Martin Stevens and sister Jade. This photograph was taken before the front room went into serious changes, the family spent next to nothing to clean the room up for Christmas 1994, as they were waiting for the renovations to be completed. The new bay window was the final phase.

Inside their parents home on Ripley Avenue in April 1995, from left: Michael Hope, his brother David and their sister Sylvia Stevens. At the beginning of December 1994, the workman began the wall cavities and draft-proofing. Garden fences were removed and concrete paths and drives put in place. Security Alarms were fitted and garden fences (galvanised steel) erected. They painted the outside top floor walls. All wooden frames for the windows and exterior doors were varnished and double-glazed windows put in. The final phase of the renovations were completed in May 1995.

The drop-in centre at Cedarwood Trust in September 2000. A few of the residents use the drop-in centre for help or advice, or just for a cup of tea. From left: Marguerite Peters, David Cato and Paul Marshall (Munchie).

Outside Cedarwood Avenue Centre around 1990. From left: Margaret Thompson, Elizabeth Wallis, Pamela Howells, Lilian White, Noreen Thompson, Carol Ann Belfon and her son Michael.

A leaving party for one of the workers at Horsham Grove Centre in 1993. Ken, the window cleaner, is standing at the back. In front is Dennis Marsh and Susanne McGary.

Horsham Grove Centre Mind Group in 1995. From left: Harry Taylor, Karen Graham and unknown.

In 1998 a group of local women went to Garrigill near Alston for a week. Their camp was a tepee and the cooking facilities were over a camp fire. A few of the activities were: painting stones, making dream-catchers, swimming and site-seeing. The weather was hot and they had problems with midges. One of the women had to break her holidays because she was quite ill with midge bites. The waterfall was a haven when they wanted to cool off. From left: Georgina Adriaansen, who was a friend from Ascot, Reverend Sheila Auld, Karen Graham and Elaine Andrews.

The Waterville Project for children and young people was established in 1993. Since that date, the project has worked with more than 1,000 young people. Originally situated in Percy Main, the project moved to The Meadows Community Centre, and are now ensconced in 35 Avon Avenue. The photograph was taken in September 2000 by Steve Elliot, one of the workers. From left: John Carmichael, Ella Bucman, Steve Conlan, Maurice Bransfield, Paul Robson, Monkey the dog and Anne Stark.

A local group of young people involved in the Waterville Detached Project are on a 'working residential' – helping members of the National Trust in the Lake District in October 2000. Back: Lee Hamilton, David Bell, Craig Miller, Susan Davies, Emma Buglass, Simon (National Trust worker) and Claire Bell. Front: Mark (National Trust worker), Stacy Dunn, Kenneth Robson and Ryan O'Neil.

Spring

by Rob Michael

Who is this beautiful virgin that approaches,

clothed in a robe of light green?

She has a garland of flowers on her head,

and flowers spring up, wherever she sets her foot.

The snow which covers the fields,

and the ice upon the rivers,

melts away when she breathes upon them.

The young lambs frisk about her,

and the birds warble to welcome her coming.

When they see her,

they begin to choose their mates and build their nests.

Youths and maidens,

have you seen this beautiful creature?

If you have,

tell me who she is and what is her name.

Right: Robert Michael in Iona in Scotland in 1997.

The Hackworth family, taken on Waterville Road in October 2000. The adults are: Karen, Karen (grandma) and Lindsey. The children are: Joanne, Nichola, Robert, Danielle, Jordan, Cuthbert, Ashleigh, Leon Hackworth and baby Scott Ashcroft.